AR Level
BL: 3.5
Pts: 0.5

First
Facts®

ELITE MILITARY FORCES

THE ARMY RANGERS

by Jennifer M. Besel

Consultants:
Tracy A. Bailey, Public Affairs Officer, 75th Ranger Regiment
U.S. Army Special Operations Command, Fort Benning, Georgia

Lisa C. Moore, Public Affairs Specialist, U.S. Army Special Operations Command
Public Affairs Office, Fort Bragg, North Carolina

CAPSTONE PRESS
a capstone imprint

First Facts is published by Capstone Press,
151 Good Counsel Drive, P.O. Box 669, Mankato, Minnesota 56002.
www.capstonepub.com

Books published by Capstone Press are manufactured with paper
containing at least 10 percent post-consumer waste.

Library of Congress Cataloging-in-Publication Data
Besel, Jennifer M.
  The Army Rangers / by Jennifer M. Besel.
    p. cm. — (First facts. Elite military forces)
  Includes bibliographical references and index.
  Summary: "Provides information on the U.S. Army Rangers, including their training,
missions, and equipment"—Provided by publisher.
  ISBN 978-1-4296-5381-7 (library binding)
  1. United States. Army—Commando troops—Juvenile literature. I. Title.
  UA34.R36B46 2011
  356'.1670973—dc22   2010029383

Editorial credits:
Christine Peterson, editor; Matt Bruning, designer; Laura Manthe, production specialist

Photo credits:
DEFENSEIMAGERY.MIL, 17(machine gun); Shutterstock/Oleg Zabielin, cover; U.S.
Air Force photo by Master Sgt. Cecilio Ricardo, 13, Senior Airman Julianne Showalter,
5; U.S. Army photo, 18; U.S. Navy photo, 17(rifle); U.S. Army Special Operations
Command, 15, Sgt. Daniel Love, 7th SFG(A) PAO, 7, 8, 11, 21

Artistic Effects
iStockphoto/Brett Charlton, Craig DeBourbon; Shutterstock/koh sze kiat, Maksym
Bondarchuk, Masonjar, Péter Gudella, reventon2527, Serg64, Tom Grundy

Printed in the United States of America in North Mankato, Minnesota.
042011   006171R

TABLE OF CONTENTS

ON A MISSION

Under the cover of darkness, MC-130 aircraft soar through the sky. Inside the planes, U.S. Army Rangers prepare to jump. Their parachutes carry them silently into the Afghanistan desert. The Rangers' goal is to take over a **Taliban** airfield.

Taliban: an army in Afghanistan that uses terror to spread its ideas

The Rangers move quickly. With night-vision goggles and guns ready, they overtake the enemy. The airfield is under Ranger control within hours.

Army Rangers are highly trained, **dedicated** soldiers. They defend their country against enemies anywhere in the world.

dedicated: completely committed to something, such as an idea, belief, or goal

FACT

Rangers can be ready to fight anywhere in the world within 18 hours.

FACT

U.S. Army Rangers live by the phrase, "Rangers lead the way!"

LEADING THE WAY

U.S. Army Rangers are among the world's most highly trained soldiers. They are often the first U.S. soldiers called to fight in enemy **territory**. Rangers surprise the enemy and fight in face-to-face battles. They clear the way for the rest of the Army.

territory: an area of land controlled by a country or group

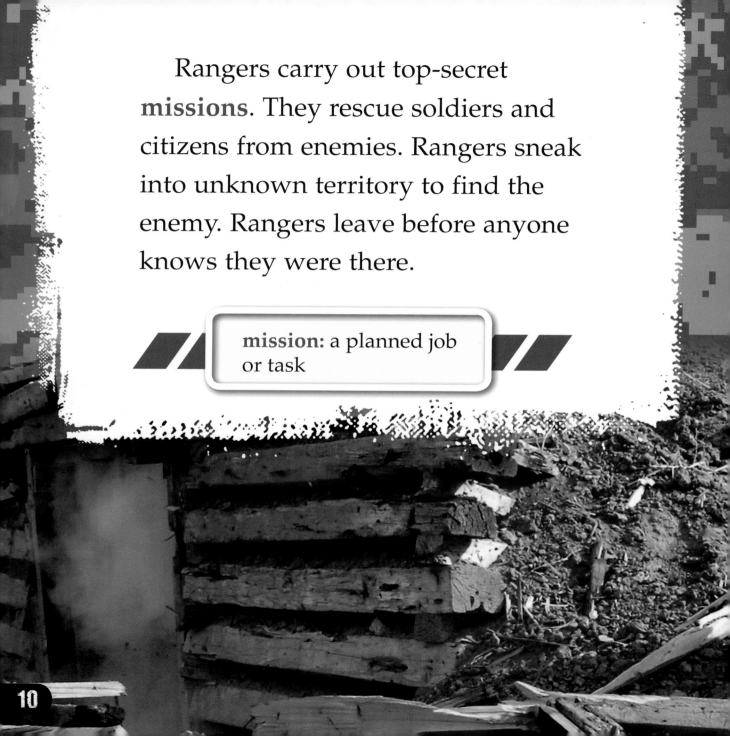

Rangers carry out top-secret **missions**. They rescue soldiers and citizens from enemies. Rangers sneak into unknown territory to find the enemy. Rangers leave before anyone knows they were there.

mission: a planned job or task

FACT

Rules made by Congress allow only men to become Rangers.

BECOMING A RANGER

Soldiers must prove they're tough enough to be Rangers. Their first test is the Ranger Assessment and Selection Program (RASP). Soldiers train at Fort Benning, Georgia. They have to pass a tough physical test. They must complete long runs and marches. Half of the soldiers who enter RASP don't finish.

FACT

Rangers are in great shape. They train five days a week, 48 weeks a year.

Those who pass RASP become members of the 75th Ranger **Regiment**. These men then attend Ranger School. At Ranger School, they train day and night. The soldiers practice hand-to-hand fighting. Soldiers crawl through swamps, learning to find enemies. They jump from helicopters and airplanes. Soldiers who pass this training become Ranger qualified.

regiment: a large group of soldiers who fight together as a unit

RANGER WEAPONS

Rangers move quickly on missions. They bring everything they need. Rangers carry M-4 carbine rifles. For heavy firepower, they bring the Ranger Anti-Armor Weapons System (RAAWS). They also use the M-249 SAW machine gun. This weapon fires 725 **rounds** per minute.

> **round:** a single bullet fired by a gun

RANGERS

M-4 carbine rifle

M-249 SAW

Ranger Ground Mobility Vehicle

FACT

During an air attack, motorcycles are put on boards attached to parachutes and dropped from planes.

Rangers use high-tech gear on missions. Night-vision goggles help soldiers see in the dark. Some missions require speed. That's when Rangers bring out the wheels. The Ranger Ground Mobility Vehicle (GMV) carries nine men into **combat**. Rangers zoom into action on motorcycles too.

combat: fighting between armies

ALWAYS PREPARED

When their nation needs help, Rangers are prepared to go. They attack by land, sea, and air. Rangers sneak unseen through mountains, deserts, and swamps. They're trained to surprise enemies or rescue soldiers. Whatever the mission, Rangers are ready to lead the way.

A Ranger's weapons and equipment can weigh up to 100 pounds (45 kilograms).

GLOSSARY

combat (KOM-bat)—fighting between people or armies

dedicated (ded-uh-KAY-tuhd)—completely committed to something, such as an idea, belief, or goal

mission (MISH-uhn)—a planned job or task

regiment (REJ-uh-muhnt)—a large group of soldiers who fight together as a unit

round (ROUND)—a single bullet fired by a gun

Taliban (TAHL-ee-bahn)—an army in Afghanistan that uses terror in an effort to spread its ideas

territory (TER-uh-tor-ee)—an area of land controlled by a country or group

READ MORE

Alvarez, Carlos. *Army Rangers*. Armed Forces. Minneapolis: Bellwether Media, 2010.

Braulick, Carrie A. *U.S. Army Rangers*. The U.S. Armed Forces. Mankato, Minn.: Capstone Press, 2006.

Sandler, Michael. *Army Rangers in Action*. Special Ops. New York: Bearport Publishing, 2008.

INTERNET SITES

FactHound offers a safe, fun way to find Internet sites related to this book. All of the sites on FactHound have been researched by our staff.

Here's all you do:

Visit *www.facthound.com*

Type in this code: 9781429653817

Check out projects, games and lots more at
www.capstonekids.com

INDEX